EXPLORING
ANCIENT ROME

by Laurie J. Edwards

12
STORY
LIBRARY

www.12StoryLibrary.com

12-Story Library is an imprint of Bookstaves and Press Room Editions

Produced for 12-Story Library by Red Line Editorial

Photographs ©: S.Borisov/Shutterstock Images, cover, 1; Andrew_Howe/iStockphoto, 4; North Wind Picture Archives, 6, 8, 11; Deposit Photos/Glow Images, 7, 28; Dea/A.Dagli Orti/De Agostini/Getty Images, 10; Dea/G.Nimatallah/De Agostini/Getty Images, 12; Fabian von Poser/ImageBroker RM/ Glow Images, 13; Simone-/iStockphoto, 14, 29; Blueplace/iStockphoto, 15; khd/Shutterstock Images, 16; DeAgostini/Superstock, 17; Alexandra Lande/Shutterstock Images, 18; XYZ Pictures/ImageBroker RM/Glow Images, 20; Aksenovko/iStockphoto, 21; BlackMac/Shutterstock Images, 22; Motordigitaal/ Shutterstock Images, 23; G.dallorto CC, 24; Lals Stock/Shutterstock Images, 25; mountainpix/ Shutterstock Images, 26; piola666/iStockphoto, 27

Content Consultant: George Houston, Professor Emeritus of Classics, The University of North Carolina at Chapel Hill

Library of Congress Cataloging-in-Publication Data
Names: Edwards, Laurie J., author.
Title: Exploring Ancient Rome / by Laurie J. Edwards.
Description: Mankato, MN : 12 Story Library, 2018. | Series: Exploring
    ancient civilizations | Includes bibliographical references and index. |
    Audience: Grades 4-6.
Identifiers: LCCN 2016047956 (print) | LCCN 2016049382 (ebook) | ISBN
    9781632354662 (hardcover : alk. paper) | ISBN 9781632355317 (pbk. : alk.
    paper) | ISBN 9781621435839 (hosted e-book)
Subjects: LCSH: Rome--Civilization--Juvenile literature. |
    Rome--History--Juvenile literature.
Classification: LCC DG77 .E39 2018 (print) | LCC DG77 (ebook) | DDC 937--dc23
LC record available at https://lccn.loc.gov/2016047956

Printed in the United States of America
032017

Access free, up-to-date content on this topic plus a full digital version of this book. Scan the QR code on page 31 or use your school's login at 12StoryLibrary.com.

Table of Contents

Rome Was Built Over Hundreds of Years

Over the course of 1,200 years, the Romans built an empire. The Roman Empire started small. Eventually it became one of the largest empires in history. It dominated the lands around the Mediterranean Sea. At its height, the empire even stretched beyond the continent of Europe. It included parts of northern Africa, the Middle East, and the isle of Great Britain.

Rome's greatest extent reached from Great Britain to the Middle East.

ROMAN EMPIRE,
IN ITS GREATEST EXTENT.
BY J. BARTHOLOMEW F.R.G.S.

21

Day in April the city of Rome was founded, according to the Roman historian Livy.

- Rome began as a small village but grew into a large empire.
- According to legend, two brothers, Romulus and Remus, built Rome. Romulus killed his brother and ruled the city.
- The ancient Romans were greatly influenced by the Greeks and Etruscans.

THINK ABOUT IT

Much of what we know about early Roman history was written down at least 600 years after the events. Stories were passed down orally. How might stories change over hundreds of years? Is what's written in history books always accurate?

Rome began as a small village. It is located in the middle of modern-day Italy. The Romans told many stories about the founding of their city. In one famous myth, twin infants, Romulus and Remus, were abandoned in a basket. The babies were found and cared for by a mother wolf. Later a shepherd found and raised them. As adults, the brothers decided to build a city. Legend says they founded Rome in 753 BCE. But the brothers argued, and Romulus killed Remus. Romulus then became the king of Rome.

Many other groups of people lived in Italy. The Etruscans lived to the north. They influenced Roman art and architecture. They taught the Romans how to build with brick and tile. The Romans also adopted some of the Etruscans' religion. Romans learned to wear togas. They based their military on the Etruscan army.

South of Rome there were several Greek cities. Some Greeks had left Greece to find new cities in Italy. The Greeks taught the Romans grape and olive farming. They shared their alphabet. Romans copied Greek architecture, literature, and art.

Many Leaders Ruled Ancient Rome

Romulus was the first king of Rome. Ancient historians say six kings ruled the city after him. They won wars against their neighbors. Rome's control in what is now Italy expanded. Stories say the seventh and last king was Tarquin the Proud. He killed the previous king and his political enemies. He oppressed the people. In 509 BCE, the people drove him from the city. After that, the kings were driven out and two officers called consuls led Rome. Consuls stayed in office for only one year. One consul could veto, or overrule, the other.

The Roman Senate worked with the consuls to rule the city and its lands. The Senate was a group of men who recommended which laws should be passed. Senators usually served for their entire lives. The republic and the Senate were dominated by wealthy, elite families, called the patricians. Common

> The Roman Senate made laws on topics ranging from religion to finance.

482
Number of years Rome was ruled by emperors.

- After the kings, Rome became a republic.
- Octavian became the first emperor and took the name Augustus Caesar.
- Rome had many emperors.

people were called plebeians. They had their own assemblies that also made laws. Two officials called tribunes of the plebs stood up for plebeian rights.

Civil wars occurred in the first century BCE. Generals fought for control. Then Julius Caesar came to power. The senators feared he was too powerful. They murdered him in 44 BCE. More wars followed as several generals fought for power. Octavian was the victor. He was Julius Caesar's grand-nephew and heir. He became emperor in 27 BCE and took the name Augustus Caesar.

After Augustus Caesar, many emperors followed. Some emperors were good and ruled for the good of Rome. Others wanted power, glory, or wealth for themselves. The Senate lost power. Meanwhile the empire grew.

Augustus ruled until his death in 14 CE.

ROMAN LAW

Rome had a large body of written laws. It grew larger over time. Laws governed business deals and contracts. Other laws set punishments for crimes. During the early republic, the Twelve Tables laid out the rights of citizens. The Senate, assemblies of the people, and the emperor all could make laws. They could adapt the laws to special circumstances. Law experts called jurists debated the laws and reinterpreted them. They wanted the laws to be fair and practical.

Rome Became a Great Military Power

The might of the Roman republic, and later the empire, was its army. Roman soldiers were well trained. Rome's navy protected the coast. The military fought many wars and conquered other lands.

Between 400 and 200 BCE, Rome slowly conquered the

rest of Italy. The conquered cities and tribes came under Rome's control. Eventually, many of these people became citizens of Rome. Male citizens had a voice in the government and could vote in elections. Female citizens were not allowed to vote. Italian soldiers increased the size of Rome's armies.

The first Punic War lasted from 264 BCE to 241 BCE.

During the republic, one of Rome's major enemies was Carthage. Carthage was in North Africa. The two powers fought for control of the Mediterranean Sea. The three major conflicts are called the Punic Wars. They began in 264 BCE. Fighting ended in 146 BCE. Rome gained power, money, and access to trade routes.

As Rome became an empire, the army grew more powerful. It conquered more distant lands. Rome had enemies on all sides. It was always at war on its frontiers.

Conquering soldiers brought goods and slaves back to the capital. Later, some people in conquered lands became citizens of Rome.

A legion was an army unit. Each legion had approximately 5,500 men. Members of the cavalry rode horses. They led soldiers into battle. Foot soldiers and archers followed them. Soldiers wore heavy armor and carried large shields. They used spears and swords. A Roman army camp was highly organized. It was always set up the same way. The square camp was surrounded by ditches for protection. The tents were pitched in straight lines. The general's tent, the supplies, the horses—everything had its specific placement.

60
Weight in pounds (27 kg) of a Roman soldier's pack.

- Rome built a strong army. The legions were highly organized.
- The borders of Rome kept expanding. Soldiers brought treasure and slaves back to Rome.
- Some conquered people eventually became citizens of Rome.

THINK ABOUT IT

What are some advantages of always organizing the army's camp in the same way? Are there any drawbacks?

Roman Society Was Diverse but Divided

Roman society was divided by class. During the republic, wealthy patrician families held most of the political power. During the empire, the patricians lost power. The emperor and his family were at the top. The senators still had some influence, but the Senate was not as powerful as it once was.

Below was the equestrian class. Many equestrians were wealthy business people. Some were foreigners. They worked in the military and in the government.

The wealthiest and most talented could become senators. The common people, plebeians, were mostly farmers. There were also craftspeople, tradespeople, and soldiers.

As Rome expanded, Italians and people from more distant lands came under Roman control. Some became citizens. Some moved to Rome, which was filled with people from far-flung lands. Some joined the army. Their ideas, cultures,

This sculpture shows Roman men shopping for fabric.

and religions mixed with Roman traditions.

Many foreigners came to Rome as slaves. They were prisoners of war or slaves bought outside Roman territory. Sometimes very poor Romans sold their children into slavery. Wealthy people owned many slaves. Slaves farmed the land. They worked in houses and shops. Slaves who were trusted managed money. Some became teachers, architects, or doctors. But many slaves were treated badly. A slave owner could kill a slave without punishment.

Slaves could earn their freedom. Freed slaves were skilled, so they could support themselves. Many still worked for their masters. Freedmen had rights, but they could not hold office. They faced social discrimination, or unfair treatment. Their children were born free, full citizens, however.

Wealthy Romans had many feasts.

400,000
Number of sesterces (coins) a Roman citizen had to own to be considered an equestrian.

- The senatorial class was the highest-ranking, and its members were very wealthy.
- Equestrians worked in business, the military, and the government. Plebeians worked in shops, trades, and farms.
- There were many slaves in Rome, and they did many different jobs. Slaves could earn their freedom.

THINK ABOUT IT

Research two Roman jobs. Make a chart. Compare and contrast them. Which one would you rather do? Why?

Fathers Ruled Roman Families

Roman men were in charge of their families. Wives and children obeyed them. The head of the family was called the paterfamilias. He controlled his children and their families, too. He had the power of life and death over his family and his slaves.

Most women were homemakers. They cared for children. They kept the house running smoothly.

Poor women worked in shops. Some worked as hairdressers. Others were dressmakers. A few practiced medicine. Baby girls were called by their father's middle name. For example, Gaius Julius Caesar's daughter was Julia. Two daughters would be called *major* and *minor* (big and little) or *prima* and *secunda* (first and second).

> Roman children played with animal figurines and wheeled toys.

14

Age at which a boy began wearing a toga and registered as a Roman citizen.

- Fathers ruled the family. Most women were homemakers.
- Wealthy children went to school at age seven. Poor children worked.
- Arranged marriages increased a family's wealth or social standing.

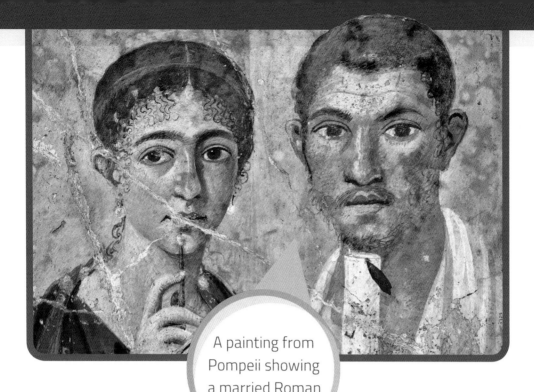

A painting from Pompeii showing a married Roman couple

Roman children played games. They had dolls and pull toys. Boys had hoops and tops. They built with bricks. Mothers taught their children at home. By age seven, wealthy children went to school. They learned to read and write Latin. Boys and girls studied together. They wrote on wax tablets. Lessons included Greek and arithmetic. Poor children went to work. Some became apprentices. An expert taught them their jobs. Slaves worked from a young age.

Girls could marry at age 12. Boys could marry at age 14. But most grooms were much older than the brides. Usually fathers arranged the marriage. A good marriage increased the family's wealth or social standing. Weddings occurred at the bride's home. The bride wore a white tunic. Her veil and shoes were flame-colored. The couple held hands during the ceremony. A sacrifice came next. Then they had a feast. Everyone went to the groom's house. The bride was carried over the threshold. This was for good luck.

Divorces were easy. The couple said they would not live together. Then the woman went back home. Or she lived independently.

Romans Were Master Builders

The Romans built to last. Many monuments, roads, and walls that the Romans built still exist today. Straight roads connected most of the empire. Romans developed concrete. This let them construct large buildings, such as the Colosseum, a giant amphitheater. Many buildings featured arches, domes, and vaults. Vaults are curved ceilings. Romans built the Pantheon, a temple, in the 120s CE. It had the largest dome in the world at the time it was built. It has remained standing for almost 2,000 years.

Romans are known for aqueducts. These channels piped water into the city. Some were built high in the air on a series of arches. Aqueducts allowed the city's population to soar.

These ancient ruins stand in the city of Jerash, Jordan. The city used to be called Gerasa when it was under Roman rule.

The Pantheon is now used as a Catholic church.

Much of Rome's population squeezed into apartment buildings called insulae. Apartment buildings might have been 70 feet (20 m) tall. Some of them were not well constructed. Tenants feared fires, floods, and collapsing buildings. Town houses called *domus* were single-family homes. Most of them had atriums, or central courtyards, with rooms all around. The ceiling was open overhead. It let in sun and rain. A pool below the opening collected rainwater.

Rich people had large country homes. These villas had atriums. They also had gardens. Many rooms surrounded the atrium. Villas might have had under-floor heating. Some had running water and indoor bathrooms. Owners decorated the walls of most rooms. They used murals or mosaics. Mosaics were made with tiny square tiles of stone, glass, or pottery. They formed pictures or patterns.

46,000
Number of apartment buildings in Rome in the early fourth century CE.

- Romans developed the use of concrete and used arches and vaults to construct long-lasting structures.
- The poor often lived in cramped apartments, which were poorly built.
- The wealthy owned large villas that had indoor baths and running water.

15

Romans Liked to Shop, Eat, and Dress Up

Shops and stalls jammed busy Roman streets. Chattering monkeys and caged animals attracted buyers. People purchased food, clothing, and goods from faraway lands. Hungry customers stopped at fast food stands. They bought hot sausages, chickpeas, or pastries. People added pepper, spices, and fish sauce to their food. At home, the basic Roman diet included bread or porridge, olives and olive oil, grapes, wine, and fruits and vegetables.

Wealthy people held fancy banquets. Guests reclined on sloping couches. They ate with knives, spoons, and their fingers. Slaves washed the guests' hands during the meal. Slaves also sang and danced. Some did magic or acrobatics.

A Roman's clothing told much about his or her social class. Men wore the toga. This large piece of white wool cloth was draped around the body. The style, color, and stripes showed a person's rank. It was hot and difficult to move in. Wealthy and important men wore the toga every day. All citizens wore the toga for important events and ceremonies, but most wore a more practical tunic for work. Slaves and foreigners were not allowed to wear the toga. Women wore a floor-length tunic. Married women added an overtunic called a *stola*. Fashionable women showed their wealth through their jewelry and hairstyles.

Romans stored oil and wine in pottery jugs called *amphorae.*

100

Limit of weight in pounds (45 kg) of silver tableware allowed at a banquet, according to a 161 BCE law that was intended to cut back on excess luxury.

- Romans ate a variety of foods, and the wealthy hosted lavish banquets.
- Clothing, jewelry, and hair styles showed a person's social status.
- Male citizens wore tunics, togas, or both.

ROMAN RECIPES

The Romans used some unusual ingredients in their beauty treatments. To stop balding, they rubbed ashes of hippopotamus skin onto their heads. They covered their gray hair with a concoction of boiled walnut shells, earthworms, and ashes. They made black hair dye by letting leeches rot for 40 days in wine. And some whitened their teeth by brushing them with urine. They also used urine to clean clothes.

Wealthy women spent hours on beauty. Slaves applied their cosmetics. They used chalk and lead to whiten their mistresses' faces. The Romans did not know lead was poisonous. Next came rouge. Wine made cheeks pink. Hairdressers fixed elaborate styles.

People gathered at public baths. These buildings provided areas to exercise and relax. They had large pools. People used them for bathing. While they bathed, they talked with friends.

Freeborn Roman boys wore pendants called *bulla* to ward off evil and show their social status.

Romans Enjoyed Bloody Games

Romans rose early in the morning. They worked from dawn until noon. Then they enjoyed their afternoons. Many people looked for entertainment. Chariot races and gladiator fights were popular. People also attended the theater. Politicians and emperors paid for the entertainments to keep the common people happy.

Chariot races were held in the Circus Maximus. This enormous arena held 250,000 people. The event began with a parade. Government officials came first. Priests and priestesses followed. Next came the charioteers. Four teams—Greens, Reds, Blues, Whites—raced. People cheered for their favorite team.

Bloody fights occurred in amphitheaters throughout the empire. Romans everywhere watched gladiator fights. The large Colosseum in Rome held 50,000

The Colosseum is the largest amphitheater in the world.

GLADIATORS

Many gladiators fought with swords or knives. The word gladiator comes from their sword, the *gladius*. But some carried more unusual weapons. The *retiarius* was another type of gladiator. They used *iaculum*, a weighted net that was used to tie up his opponent. He carried a three-pronged spear called a trident in his other hand. The *laquearii* lassoed the other gladiators. Often a quick, unarmored gladiator faced off against a slower opponent with heavy armor.

people. The open arena had an overhead awning. It protected viewers from the sun. Underneath the building, cages held wild animals. Elevators with pulleys lifted the animals and fighters.

Romans captured wild animals. They brought them to the arena. Crocodiles snapped at other animals. Lions and leopards attacked and killed. Elephants, bears, or rhinos fought each other. People also fought animals. Most fights ended in death.

Later in the day, wild animals fought criminals. The animals usually won, because the criminals were not given good weapons. Then gladiators battled. Many were slaves. Others were criminals or war captives. Some were trained and paid. Women competed too. Music accompanied the fights. Some gladiators lived to fight again, but many died. Very successful gladiators could become famous.

3.5 million
Estimated number of people killed in Roman arenas.

- Public games were popular events.
- Chariot racing was the most popular sport.
- Bloody fights were held in the Colosseum.
- Most gladiators were criminals, slaves, and prisoners of war.

Romans Influenced Art and Science

Romans borrowed from other cultures. Then they added their own ideas. For example, they copied Greek methods of making statues. Greek statues showed only beautiful people. But Romans made their statues realistic. They showed warts and wrinkles.

A lot of Roman writing survives today. Authors such as Cicero, Catullus, Juvenal, and Livy wrote speeches, poetry, jokes, and history. Roman scientists wrote about agriculture, architecture, astronomy, and medicine. They improved mathematics, constructed monumental buildings, and invented new farming tools. Roman engineers created bigger and more accurate artillery. They also used their engineering skills to put on marvelous shows. Hidden trapdoors let animals and actors enter amphitheaters. Engineers may have even been able to flood the Colosseum to host battles between small ships.

Roman engineers invented flushing toilets. They built public bathrooms. Long stone benches had holes every few feet. These holes served

Romans made their art extremely realistic.

Public bathrooms in ancient Rome weren't separated by doors and stalls like they are today.

as toilets. People sat beside each other. Water flowed under the toilets to flush away the waste. The running water came from aqueducts. The waste drained into huge sewers. Romans get credit for sewers, too. The sewers helped keep city streets cleaner.

7

Number of sewers that drained waste from the ancient city of Rome.

- Roman art was realistic.
- Roman writings survive today, including works of poetry, history, and science.
- Romans created sewers and flushing toilets.

KEEPING TIME

In the early republic, the Roman calendar had 12 months that matched the moon's cycle. But this system only had 355 days. Over time, the months shifted. Harvest festivals were happening before the crops were harvested. Julius Caesar reordered the calendar. He ordered an extra-long year to catch up. He added days to some months. And he even added an extra day every four years—the leap year—to keep the calendar on track over time. The month of July was renamed in his honor. August was named after Augustus Caesar.

10

Romans Worshipped Many Gods and Goddesses

Early Romans worshipped many gods and goddesses. People asked gods for help. They thought gods sent rain and helped crops grow. Romans prayed and made sacrifices. Government officials were in charge of keeping traditions. They hosted ceremonies in honor of the gods. Priests and priestesses tended temples and altars. During the empire, emperors were regarded as gods in some eastern provinces.

Families had altars for their household gods. These spirits were the lares. They protected families. Fathers offered food to the gods. They wanted to keep their families safe.

The Romans blended different religions. They adopted Etruscan gods. They accepted Greek gods. When Rome conquered other lands, people of many cultures lived in the empire. Rome let these people keep their religion. But they had to honor the official Roman gods, too. Gods and religious sects spread from one end of the empire to the other.

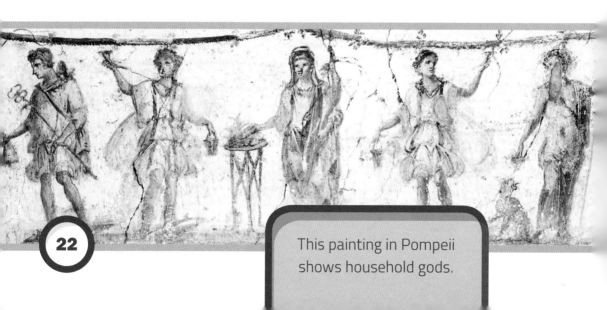

This painting in Pompeii shows household gods.

The Temple of Saturn was built to worship the god Saturn and still stands today.

Christianity arose in the first century CE. Over the next centuries, it spread despite persecution. Christians refused to honor the state gods or sacrifice to them. Roman authorities associated Christianity with civil unrest. Many early Christians were killed in an effort to stamp out the new religion. But Christianity grew and spread. In 313 CE, the emperor lifted laws against Christians. By the 400s CE, Christianity was the official religion.

CURSE TABLETS

The Romans believed their gods listened to their requests. They asked the gods to curse their enemies or other people who wronged them. They wrote a curse on a sheet of lead. The writer promised to give the god some kind of gift. Then the tablet was folded up and dropped in a deep well, river, or spring, or was buried. Sometimes the curse came true. Then people had to keep their promises to the gods.

30

Years a priestess called a Vestal Virgin served without marrying while tending to the Temple of Vesta, goddess of the hearth.

- Romans had many gods and goddesses.
- Rome accepted other religions and gods.
- Early Christians were persecuted, but Christianity spread anyway.

The Roman Empire Broke Apart

The Roman Empire reached its largest size in 117 CE. After that, the emperors' focus shifted from expanding to protecting the borders. But it was difficult to rule the giant empire. In 284, Emperor Diocletian split the empire between four leaders. The empire split into eastern and western parts. The western capital remained in Rome. The eastern capital was in Byzantium, which is modern-day Istanbul.

Germanic tribes had attacked the border along the Rhine River since Julius Caesar's time. Some emperors fought them, and some paid them off. Others invited them to settle in the empire. They would fight off outside tribes. But the settled Germans kept their own culture.

Constant warfare was expensive. It disrupted trade. Battles ruined crops. A lack of food and money put Rome in a downward spiral. The government became unstable. A German tribe, the Visigoths, sacked the city in 410 CE. Other groups conquered pieces of the empire until only Italy remained in all of the western half of the empire.

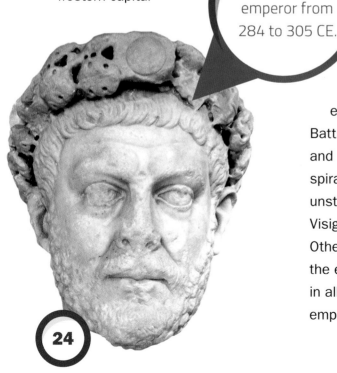

Diocletian was emperor from 284 to 305 CE.

The Roman Empire fell in 476 CE when the German commander Odovacar took control of the city of Rome. He dethroned the last emperor and called himself king of Italy. Europe became a patchwork of cities and kingdoms, each with its own rulers. The Byzantine Empire continued in the east until the Ottoman Turks conquered Byzantium in 1453.

1.9

Area in million square miles (4 million sq km) of the empire's largest extent.

- The Roman Empire divided into eastern and western parts.
- Constant warfare drained Rome's economy.
- German and other European tribes conquered the old empire and the city of Rome itself by 476 CE.

Constantinople, formerly Byzantium, was made the capital of the eastern half of the Roman Empire by Emperor Constantine in 324 CE.

The Roman Empire Lived On

The Roman Empire had ended. But Roman inventions and ideas remained. They spread around the world. The Byzantine emperor Justinian simplified Roman law in the 500s CE. The Code of Justinian was the basis of the law in the old Roman Empire for centuries to come.

The works of the ancient Romans are still studied today. They still influence modern Western literature. The Romans' Latin language was used for science and education for centuries. Modern Romance languages such as Italian, Spanish, and French have Latin roots.

Christianity was spread throughout the Roman Empire. The religion

Justinian I ruled from 527 to 565 CE.

The influence of the Roman Empire has lasted thousands of years.

became the most powerful institution in Europe in the Middle Ages. The headquarters of the western church remained in Rome. Today the Catholic Church's leader, the Pope, still lives in Rome.

Romans developed roads, engineering methods, plumbing, and concrete. Their roads and buildings were built to last. Roman roads still linked European kingdoms through the Middle Ages. Stretches of Roman roads exist today. All of those and more have been Rome's gift to the world.

920 million

Number of people who speak a Romance language as their first language in the 2000s.

- Roman law governed in the old Roman Empire for centuries.
- Ancient Roman works are read and studied today, and many modern languages have Latin roots.
- The Catholic Church rose to power in Europe after the fall of Rome.
- Roman roads and buildings still stand today.

12 Key Dates

753 BCE
Rome is founded.

509 BCE
The rule of kings ends. The republic begins.

400–200 BCE
Rome slowly conquers the rest of Italy.

264–146 BCE
Rome fights Carthage in the Punic Wars. Rome's army continues to grow.

44 BCE
Julius Caesar is ruler of Rome. He is then murdered for fear of being too powerful.

27 BCE
Octavian takes over Rome. The rule of the emperors begins.

117 CE
The Roman Empire reaches its largest size and power.

120s CE
Romans build the Pantheon, their large temple, which has remained standing for almost 2,000 years.

284 CE

Emperor Diocletian divides the empire between four leaders because of its size. The empire is split into eastern and western parts.

410 CE

The Visigoths sack the city of Rome. Rome slowly becomes unstable.

476 CE

The Roman Empire ends. The Eastern half survives. It is called the Byzantine Empire.

1453

Byzantium is conquered by the Ottoman Turks. The Byzantine Empire ends.

Glossary

amphitheater
An open oval building with seating for viewers to watch events.

aqueduct
A manmade channel or pipe for supplying water.

atrium
An entrance hall with an open roof.

consuls
The two top government officials in the Roman republic.

empire
A government ruled by an emperor.

freedmen
Slaves who became free.

gladiator
A person trained to fight other people or animals in an arena.

legion
The largest unit of the Roman army.

patricians
Wealthy landowners who were Roman citizens; usually had political influence.

persecute
To hurt, harass, or kill someone because of their beliefs.

plebeians
Roman citizens who were not patricians.

republic
A government in which the people and their elected representatives hold the power.

toga
Clothing of a Roman citizen; a long piece of cloth that draped around the body and over the shoulder.

For More Information

Books

England, Victoria. *Top 10 Worst Things about Ancient Rome You Wouldn't Want to Know!* New York: Gareth Stevens Publishing, 2012.

Greenwood, Mary, et al, eds. *DK Findout! Ancient Rome.* New York: DK Children, 2016.

Hardyman, Robyn. *Horrible Jobs in Ancient Greece and Rome.* New York: Gareth Stevens Publishing, 2014.

Klar, Jeremy. *The Totally Gross History of Ancient Rome.* New York: Rosen, 2016.

Visit 12StoryLibrary.com

Scan the code or use your school's login at **12StoryLibrary.com** for recent updates about this topic and a full digital version of this book. Enjoy free access to:

- Digital ebook
- Breaking news updates
- Live content feeds
- Videos, interactive maps, and graphics
- Additional web resources

Note to educators: Visit 12StoryLibrary.com/register to sign up for free premium website access. Enjoy live content plus a full digital version of every 12-Story Library book you own for every student at your school.

Index

About the Author

A former teacher and librarian, Laurie J. Edwards is a freelance author, editor, and illustrator. In addition to having more than 2,300 magazine and educational articles published, she is the author of 36 books in print or forthcoming under several pen names.

32

READ MORE FROM 12-STORY LIBRARY

Every 12-Story Library book is available in many formats. For more information, visit 12StoryLibrary.com.